Endorsements for the Church Questions Series

"Christians are pressed by very real questions. How does Scripture structure a church, order worship, organize ministry, and define biblical leadership? Those are just examples of the questions that are answered clearly, carefully, and winsomely in this new series from 9Marks. I am so thankful for this ministry and for its incredibly healthy and hopeful influence in so many faithful churches. I eagerly commend this series."

R. Albert Mohler Jr., President, The Southern Baptist Theological Seminary

"Sincere questions deserve thoughtful answers. If you're not sure where to start in answering these questions, let this series serve as a diving board into the pool. These minibooks are winsomely to-the-point and great to read together with one friend or one hundred friends."

Gloria Furman, author, *Missional Motherhood* and *The Pastor's Wife*

"As a pastor, I get asked lots of questions. I'm approached by unbelievers seeking to understand the gospel, new believers unsure about next steps, and maturing believers wanting help answering questions from their Christian family, friends, neighbors, or coworkers. It's in these moments that I wish I had a book to give them that was brief, answered their questions, and pointed them in the right direction for further study. Church Questions is a series that provides just that. Each booklet tackles one question in a biblical, brief, and practical manner. The series may be called Church Questions, but it could be called 'Church Answers.' I intend to pick these up by the dozens and give them away regularly. You should too."

Juan R. Sanchez, Senior Pastor, High Pointe Baptist Church, Austin, Texas

Why Should I Join a Church?

Church Questions

Why Should I
Join a Church?

Mark Dever

WHEATON, ILLINOIS

Trade paperback ISBN: 978-1-4335-6815-2
ePub ISBN: 978-1-4335-6818-3
PDF ISBN: 978-1-4335-6816-9
Mobipocket ISBN: 978-1-4335-6817-6

Library of Congress Cataloging-in-Publication Data

Names: Dever, Mark, author.
Title: Why should I join a church? / Mark Dever.
Description: Wheaton: Crossway, 2020. | Series: Church questions
Identifiers: LCCN 2019025541 (print) | LCCN 2019025542 (ebook) | ISBN 9781433568152 (paperback) | ISBN 9781433568169 (pdf) | ISBN 9781433568176 (mobi) | ISBN 9781433568183 (epub)
Subjects: LCSH: Church membership.
Classification: LCC BV820 .D38 2020 (print) | LCC BV820 (ebook) | DDC 262—dc23
LC record available at https://lccn.loc.gov/2019025541
LC ebook record available at https://lccn.loc.gov/2019025542

Crossway is a publishing ministry of Good News Publishers.

BP		31	30	29	28	27	26	25	24	23	22	21
14	13	12	11	10	9	8	7	6	5	4	3	2

A new command I give to you: Love one another. As I have loved you, so you must love one another. By this all men will know that you are my disciples, if you love one another.

John 13:34–35

Sometimes college campus ministries will ask me to speak to their students. I've been known, on several occasions, to begin my remarks this way: "If you call yourself a Christian but you are not a member of the church you regularly attend, you might be going to hell."

You could say that it gets their attention.

Now, am I just going for shock value? I don't think so. Am I trying to scare them into church membership? Not really. Am I saying that joining a church makes someone a Christian? Certainly not! Throw any book (or speaker) out the window that says as much.

So why would I begin with this kind of warning? It's because I want them to see something of the urgency of the need for a healthy local church in a Christian's life and to begin sharing the passion for the church that characterizes both Christ and his followers. I want them to see that, for the sake of their souls, they need to join a local church.

If you want to follow Christ but aren't a member of a local church, consider with me seven reasons why you should join one.

1) Join a Church to Display the Gospel

In more than twenty years of pastoral ministry, I've met dozens of folks who are skeptical about the idea of church membership. After all, Christianity is about a personal relationship with God through Jesus Christ, not about attaching your name to a piece of paper or engaging in church business meetings. In fact, why waste time talking about church membership when we could be talking about Jesus? For some folks, the very idea of church membership seems like a distraction from what should be the most important thing in our lives—the gospel.

I agree, of course, that all Christians should make the gospel the center of their lives. We want to share the gospel with others and see it advance throughout the world. We want our lives to reflect the love of God in the gospel and, as Paul said, walk in a manner "worthy of the gospel of Christ" (Phil. 1:27). I'm passionate that every Christian display the gospel in their lives, which is why I'm passionate about church membership.

Church membership wasn't invented by pastors, ministry leaders, or church growth experts. Membership is the natural outcome of the gospel itself. Perhaps you've never considered it, but the gospel is not just about how God saves us *from* the "dominion of darkness"; it's also a message about how God saves us *into* the "kingdom of the Son he loves"—a kingdom bustling with other redeemed sinners who, like us, are now citizens of heaven (Col. 1:13; see also Eph. 2:19). If you're passionate about the gospel, then one of the primary ways you display the gospel to the world is by joining a local church. Let's unpack that idea.

The gospel is a message about how guilty sinners can be reconciled to a holy God through the death and resurrection of Christ. Christians are those who recognize their own moral bankruptcy and, repenting of sin, turn to Christ for forgiveness. Declared righteous in Christ and indwelt by the Holy Spirit, they now gladly live under the rule of Christ, following his commands and seeking to glorify God. Ultimately, a Christian is someone who has been reconciled to God.

Yet that's not all! The gospel not only reconciles us to God but also to his people. One reason so many Christians have minimized the importance of church membership is because they've reduced the gospel to *merely* a personal relationship with God and not much else. But the Bible teaches something quite different.

Sinners are hostile not only to God, but to those who bear his image. Our broken relationship with God creates broken relationships with others. The Bible regularly portrays that reality. In fact, do you remember the first story in the Bible after Adam and Eve's fall and banishment from the garden? It's the story of one human being murdering another—Cain killing Abel. Sinners want to shove God off his throne and put themselves on it, and, as Cain shows, we're not about to let some other human being take it from us. Not a chance. Adam's act of breaking fellowship with God resulted in an immediate break in fellowship among all human beings. It's every man for himself.

Thus, when the gospel restores our relationship with God, it also restores fellowship between us and other redeemed sinners. When we abandon our hostility toward God, we also abandon our hostility for one another. In other words, Christians are those who now delight in the great commandment: Love the Lord your God with all your heart, soul, and mind and love your neighbor as yourself (Matt. 22:34–40). What does the gospel produce in us? Love for God and love for his people.

Being reconciled to God, then, means being reconciled to everyone else who is reconciled to God. This point isn't merely an inference of the gospel message. Jesus and the apostles explicitly and frequently teach this idea throughout the New Testament.

For instance, in the first half of Ephesians 2, Paul describes the salvation Christ has provided for his people. Many Christians rightly treasure Paul's words that we are saved "by grace . . . through faith" and as a "gift of God—not by works" (Eph. 2:8–9). Yet, after showing how the gospel restores our fellowship with God, Paul turns, in the second half of Ephesians 2, to show how the gospel restores fellowship between all those who are in Christ:

> For he himself is our peace, who has made the two one and has destroyed the barrier, the dividing wall of hostility. . . . His purpose was to create in himself one new man out of the two, thus making peace, and in this one body to reconcile both of them to God through the cross, by which he put to death their hostility. (Eph. 2:14–16)

All those who belong to God are "fellow citizens" and "members of God's household" (v. 19).

Christ has destroyed our "hostility" toward one another. In Christ, God's people have "peace" and are reconciled into "one body." Paul's words are inescapably clear: if we're reconciled to God, we're reconciled to his people.

Yes, the gospel gives us a personal relationship with God. But according to Scripture, that relationship with God includes meaningful relationships with his people. When we come to Christ, he folds us into a family—a family with actual flesh-and-blood, step-on-your-toes people.

Church membership, therefore, is the natural outgrowth of the gospel. When we receive God's mercy, we become part of "a people" (1 Pet. 2:10). When we receive God's grace (Eph. 2:1–10), we are included in a covenant community (Eph. 2:11–20). Reconciled to God, reconciled to his people.

Local churches are the places where we live according to this new reality. We don't just *say* we're reconciled, we *show* it. We show it by joining a congregation and committing to love one another and help one another grow in

Christlikeness. We show it by inviting one another into our homes and caring for each other's needs. We show it by confessing our sins to one another and forgiving one another. We show it by putting aside personal preferences and considering the interests of others above our own. We show it by learning and submitting to the word of God together. By joining a church, we commit to other redeemed sinners and show the world that Christ has indeed reconciled us both to God and to each other.

It's not enough to merely have Christian friends with whom we occasionally gather—friends we pick and choose according to our own tastes. What truly displays the gospel is when we commit to love and care for a group of people that includes folks utterly unlike us. We display the gospel when we gather each week to serve people who sometimes share only one thing in common with us: Jesus. We show we are reconciled in Christ when we commit to love *those* people in *that* place—no matter what faults and foibles they may have.

If you're passionate about the gospel, join a local church.

2) Join a Church Because the Bible Requires It

The gospel itself points to our need to be vitally connected to a community of fellow brothers and sisters. But does the Bible ever explicitly mention church membership? If we display the gospel by formally committing to a local church, then shouldn't we see church membership in the New Testament?

I've heard these types of questions dozens of times. Can we really say the Bible requires church membership even though it never says, "Thou shalt join a church"?

I think we can. Let me lay out five reasons why.

New Testament Churches Kept Membership Records

True, the Bible never uses the words "thou shalt join a church," but the New Testament has plenty of evidence that the early church practiced church membership. For instance, Acts 2 records the start of the church in Jerusalem. In that passage, Peter was preaching to the crowds in Jerusalem and urging them to trust in Christ and repent of their sins (Acts 2:38). How did the people respond?

> Those who accepted his message were baptized, and about three thousand were added to their number that day. (Acts 2:41)

Notice that the early church *counted* the number of new converts who followed Christ in baptism. They were keeping records. More than that, this verse says that these three thousand believers "were added" to the church—the original 120 disciples in the upper room (Acts 1:15). The early church certainly seemed to practice church membership. They knew exactly who belonged to the congregation and how many members they had.

These three thousand men and women

didn't just get baptized and never show up again. They *acted* like church members. They regularly gathered in the temple to hear the apostles' teaching, to pray, and to celebrate the Lord's Supper (Acts 2:42, 46). They were providing for one another's needs (2:45). They were inviting one another into each other's homes (2:46). We even find the church gathering for a members' meeting to discuss how to best care for their widows (6:1–2). We see also that as this local church shared the gospel, they continued to take in more members:

> And the Lord *added to their number* daily those who were being saved. (Acts 2:47)

This church in Jerusalem continued to add more and more members, and by Acts 4:4 their congregation had grown to at least five thousand members. Later in the New Testament, we even find that churches kept lists of widows who were members of the church. The early church kept membership records. The apostles practiced church membership.

The Commands of Scripture Assume Church Membership

Have you ever noticed that it's actually impossible to obey God's commands without committing yourself to a local church? Survey the New Testament, and you'll quickly find that the Christian life is not merely about affirming the right doctrines or about pursuing individual, isolated virtues. Instead, Scripture consistently shows that the Christian life revolves around the local church—a structured community with people of different ages, ethnicities, interests, and economic backgrounds.

Consider, for instance, the following commands in Scripture and how they assume a deep and abiding relationship between fellow believers who regularly gather together in a local church. Christians are commanded:

- To love one another (John 13:34–35; 15:12–17; Rom. 12:9–10; 13:8–10; Gal. 5:14; 6:10; Eph. 1:15; 1 Pet. 1:22; 2:17; 3:8; 4:8; 1 John 3:16; 4:7–12; cf. Ps. 133)

- To seek peace and unity within their congregation (Rom. 12:16; 14:19; 1 Cor. 13:7; 2 Cor. 12:20; Eph. 4:3–6; Phil. 2:3; 1 Thess. 5:13; 2 Thess. 3:11; James 3:18; 4:11)
- To avoid all strife (Prov. 17:14; Matt. 5:9; 1 Cor. 10:32; 11:16; 2 Cor. 13:11; Phil. 2:1–3)
- To care for one another physically and spiritually (Deut. 15:7–8, 11; Matt. 25:40; John 12:8; Acts 15:36; Rom. 12:13; 15:26; 1 Cor. 16:1–2; Gal. 2:10; 6:10; Heb. 13:16; James 1:27; 1 John 3:17)
- To watch over one another and hold one another accountable (Rom. 15:14; Gal. 6:1–2; Phil. 2:3–4; 2 Thess. 3:15; Heb. 12:15; cf. Lev. 19:17; Ps. 141:5)
- To work to edify one another (1 Cor. 14:12–26; Eph. 2:21–22; 4:12–29; 1 Thess. 5:11; 1 Pet. 4:10; 2 Pet. 3:18)
- To bear with one another (Matt. 18:21–22; Mark 11:25; Rom. 15:1; Gal. 6:2; Col. 3:12), including not suing one another (1 Cor. 6:1–7)
- To pray for one another (Eph. 6:18; James 5:16)

- To keep away from those who would destroy the church (Rom. 16:17; 1 Tim. 6:3–5; Titus 3:10; 2 John 10–11)
- To reject evaluating people by worldly standards (Matt. 20:26–27; Rom. 12:10–16; James 2:1–13)
- To contend together for the gospel (Phil. 1:27; Jude 3)
- To be examples to one another (Phil. 2:1–18)

These commands assume that Christians are regularly meeting together, discipling one another, and holding one another accountable. In other words, these commands assume Christians are members of a local church. The only meaningful way to fulfill these commands is by carrying them out with a specific group of people—people with whom you regularly gather. In fact, we shouldn't miss the fact that the apostles wrote these commands to local churches and not just individual Christians.

Other commands in Scripture even more explicitly demand that we join a local church. For instance, we are called to "submit" to elders in a local congregation (Heb. 13:17). We are commanded to regularly gather with our local church in order to hear God's word and encourage others (Heb. 10:25; Acts 2:42).

If we take obedience to God seriously, we simply cannot follow Scripture's commands without being a member of a local church.

1 Corinthians 12 Teaches Church Membership

Another place in Scripture that explicitly discusses church membership is 1 Corinthians 12. In this passage, Paul refers to the believers at Corinth as "members" of the body of Christ. Churches didn't adopt the language of "membership" from dues-paying clubs like Costco or the local country club. That language comes from Paul himself.

In this passage, Paul is referring to membership in a local congregation—not just the universal church. These Christians are "members" of one body precisely because they eat the Lord's Supper together (1 Cor. 10:17) and share in one another's joys and sorrows

(1 Cor. 12:26). They're not just "members" of the universal church in some abstract sense; these are "members" of a local church—the church at Corinth.

While some Christians are uncomfortable with the idea that we *must* be a member of a local church, Paul does not share that same discomfort. Notice that Paul admonishes the Corinthians for telling one another, "I don't need you" (1 Cor. 12:21). The implication, of course, is that we do *need* one another—we need the loving care and discipline of a local congregation. If the Bible has a proof text for our obligation to join a church, it's 1 Corinthians 12:21. We need, that is, we *must* unite with brothers and sisters in the local church.

New Testament Images for the Church Imply Church Membership

Additionally, the images the biblical authors use to describe Christians and their relationship to the church in the New Testament presume that Christians are members of local churches.

Paul refers to the church as a body and to Christians as "members" of it. He refers to the church as God's "household" (1 Tim. 3:15), made up of brothers and sisters in the faith. Peter refers to Christians as "stones" that are part of a "spiritual house" (1 Pet. 2:5). He also refers to Christians as "sheep" who are part of God's "flock" (1 Pet. 2:25; 5:2).

| **New Testament Images of the Church** | |
The church is . . .	*Christians are . . .*
a body	body parts (hands, feet, eyes, etc.)
God's household	brothers and sisters
a spiritual house	stones
God's flock	sheep

These images point to the fact that God intends for his people to be united together in local churches. If we are members of the body, aren't we meant to be attached to the body? If we are God's children, aren't we meant to fellowship with our brothers and sisters in God's house?

If we are stones, aren't we supposed to be part of the building? If we are God's sheep, aren't we meant to travel with the flock?

Church Discipline Texts Assume Church Membership

Some of the strongest evidences for church membership are Scripture's explicit teachings on church discipline. Church discipline, in the narrowest sense of the term, is the act of excluding someone who professes to be a Christian from membership in the church and participation in the Lord's Supper for serious, unrepentant sin—sin he or she refuses to let go.

Church discipline is how a church protects its membership and how Christians oversee one another's faithfulness to Christ.

Jesus commanded that churches discipline unrepentant members in Matthew 18:15–18. Paul likewise commanded the Corinthian church to remove from their fellowship a man walking in unrepentant sexual sin. Other passages throughout Scripture also command that the church watch over its members by church discipline (see Gal. 6:1; 2 Thess. 3:6–15; 1 Tim. 1:20; 5:19–20; Titus 3:9–11).

By giving the church the authority to confront sin, Jesus showed that he expects his people to hold one another accountable in the local church. Following Christ is costly and challenging. The world, the devil, and the sin that remains in us try to derail our commitment to Christ. In the face of those challenges, Jesus gave local churches the right to correct us when we're unrepentant so we won't make a shipwreck of our faith (1 Tim. 1:19). Members of local churches oversee and encourage one another's faith. As Paul says, we have a responsibility to watch over one another *inside* the church, but this does not extend to unbelievers *outside* the church (1 Cor. 5:12).

Church discipline assumes church membership. The New Testament expects every Christian to link arms with others in a local church where all the members can help one another follow Christ—even if that means having our sin confronted.

Is church membership in the Bible? Absolutely. It's on every page of the New Testament because the apostles are writing to real, local churches and the members who make up those churches. The apostles never address the "lone ranger Christian" because they never conceived of the category. They never assumed anyone could be a Christian and somehow not be vitally connected to a local congregation. The idea of a Christian unattached to a local church is simply foreign to the New Testament.

3) Join a Church to Love Other Christians and Edify the Church

I once had a friend who worked for a campus Christian ministry while attending a church where I was a member. He would always slip in right after the hymns, sit there for the sermon, and then leave. I asked him one day why he didn't come for the whole service.

"Well," he said, "I don't get anything out of the rest of it."

"Have you ever thought about joining the church?" I responded.

He thought that was an absurd comment. He said, "Why would I join the church? If I join them, I think they would just slow me down spiritually."

I asked, "Have you ever considered that maybe God wants you to link arms with these people, and that perhaps even though they might slow you down a little, you might help to speed them up? Perhaps that's part of God's plan for how we're supposed to live as Christians together."

Like my friend, many people approach the local church as consumers, asking "What can this church do for me?" I've met many folks who look for a church home like they shop for a new car: "The preaching is good, the music is decent, but I sure don't like the interior of this auditorium . . . and the air conditioning has problems."

Of course, we should expect some things from our local church, such as faithful preaching and biblical doctrine. But we should never approach church as customers on the lookout for the best deal in town. We are not consumers. We're adopted children joining a family.

We've already noted above that the New Testament describes the Christian life as inescapably connected to a local congregation. God commands us to serve one another, pray for one another, live at peace with one another, be kind to one another, encourage one another, gather with one another, and build one another up with the word of God. Every Christian is commanded to use his or her spiritual gifts to "build up the church" (1 Cor. 14:12). In short, God commands us to love one another, not "with words or tongue but with actions and in truth" (1 John 3:18; see also 1 John 3:14, 16; 4:21).

Church members also have particular responsibilities toward the leaders of the church, even as the leaders do to them. Leaders in the church should be respected, held in the highest regard, and honored (Phil. 2:29; 1 Thess. 5:12–13). If Christians expect their pastor to fulfill his biblical responsibilities, church members must make themselves known to him. They must regard him as a gift from Christ sent to the church for their good. The minister of the word is a steward of God's household and an under-shepherd of God's flock. He serves willingly and eagerly (1 Pet. 5:1–3). His reputation can and should be defended, his word believed, and his instructions obeyed unless Scripture is contradicted or facts are plainly distorted (Heb. 13:17, 22; 1 Tim. 5:17–19). The faithful minister should be so regarded simply because he brings God's word to his people; he does not replace it with his own.

Church members should remember their leaders and imitate their life and faith (1 Cor. 4:16; 11:1; Phil. 3:17; Heb. 13:7). Good preachers and teachers are worthy of being doubly honored, according to Paul in 1 Timothy 5:17, which includes material support (see also Acts 6:4; 1 Cor. 9:7–14; Gal. 6:6). And church members should give themselves both to praying for their ministers and to assisting them in every way they can (Eph. 6:18–20; Col. 4:3–4; 2 Thess. 3:1; Heb. 13:18–19). Ministers of the word have been given the task of bringing God's word to God's people.

If we diagrammed all of the responsibilities God gives Christians in Scripture, it might look something like the figure on the next page.

By joining a church we *commit* to loving a particular group of people in the ways described above. Yes, we intend to love all Christians, but we "put flesh" on that intention—we put our money where our mouth is—by committing to a particular group of real people. This type of love is often difficult and inconvenient. These inconveniences are precisely why, in church membership, we covenant together to carry out this love in the good times and in the bad. The lack of commitment fostered by a lack of formal membership in a local church is a temptation to our flesh and an opportunity for self-deception. The inconveniences of love are minimized and, as a result, our love is a less compelling commendation of the gospel. Membership holds us accountable to practice true love and encourages us to love others in the way that the Bible commands.

If you consider yourself a Christian but refuse to commit to a group of people dedicated to following Jesus, I fear you may not have much reason to think you are genuinely converted. Yes, loving other believers involves all types of inconveniences and opens us up to hurt and disappointment. But truly mature Christians don't leave the church behind. They follow the Bible's commands to love their brothers and sisters and patiently endure with a particular group of redeemed sinners—even sinners who wound them. As they love, forgive, grieve, and rejoice with others in a local church, they display the love of Christ.

What about you? Do you love the people of God? Do you actually, actively give to them? Do you use your hands for them? Your money? Your lips?

In the church, discipleship is both an individual project and a corporate activity as we follow Christ and help each other along the way. We can hold each other accountable in times of temptation. We can study God's word together to prepare us for spiritual warfare. We can sing God's praises together and pray together. We can encourage each other's joy and share each other's burdens. As Jesus told us, "My command is this: Love each other as I have loved you. . . . This is my command: Love each other" (John 15:12, 17). Link arms with the other Christians around you to build the church.

4) Join a Church to Evangelize the World

It may sound odd, but one way we love non-Christians and evangelize the world is by joining a local church. By joining a church, we show non-Christians and those who think they are Christians what true conversion looks like. We provide a clear distinction between the church and the world, visibly showing that believers are "inside" the church, while unbelievers remain "outside" (1 Cor. 5:12).

Furthermore, when we join a local church, we intensify our evangelistic efforts. When we act together, we can better spread the gospel at home and abroad. We can do this by our words, as we share the good news with others and as we help others to do so. We back up this evangelistic outreach with our actions as we commend the gospel with good works.

A local church is, by nature, a missionary organization. We promote the gospel by cooperating to take it to those who have not yet heard it, and by making the gospel visible to the world through how we live.

Jesus taught that "all men" know that we are his disciples if we "love one another" (John 13:34–35). When the world looks at the church, they should see Christ's love in our care for each other. As imperfect as we are, if God's Spirit is genuinely at work in us, he will use our lives to help demonstrate to others the truth of his gospel. This is a special role we have now that we won't have in heaven—to be part of God's plan to take his gospel to the world.

Have you ever considered that the church is Jesus's evangelism plan? As we declare the message of God's love in Christ, we also display that same love in the local church. As we forgive one another, call one another to repentance, encourage one another, and speak the word of God to one another, we display the love of Christ who did these same things for us. Our lives *together* give credibility to the message we proclaim. If we truly love our non-Christian friends, we'll sign up for Jesus's evangelism plan and commit to a local congregation.

5) Join a Church to Assure Yourself

You don't join a church in order to be saved, but you may want to join the church to help you in making certain that you are saved. Remember the words of Jesus:

> Whoever has my commands and obeys them, he is the one who loves me. He who loves me will be loved by my Father, and I

too will love him and show myself to him.
. . . If you obey my commands, you will
remain in my love, just as I have obeyed
my Father's commands and remain in his
love. . . . You are my friends if you do what
I command. . . . Now that you know these
things, you will be blessed if you do them.
(John 14:21; 15:10, 14; 13:17)

I could quote many more words from Jesus
that teach us how we are to follow him and how
we must be careful not to delude ourselves. In
joining a church, we are asking our brothers and
sisters to hold us accountable to live according
to what we speak with our mouths. We ask the
brothers and sisters around us to encourage us,
sometimes by reminding us of ways that we have
seen God work in our lives and, other times, by
challenging us when we may be moving away
from obeying him.

It is easy to fool ourselves into thinking we're
Christians simply because at one time we made
a tearful decision and then joined a church. Perhaps we've gone along with the life of the church

for years, supporting its organizations, making friendships based around activities, liking some of the hymns, complaining about others, but never really knowing Christ. Do you have a vital relationship with Christ that changes your life and the lives of those around you?

How can you tell if you do? One of the ways you can discover the truth about your own life is to ask this question: Do I understand that following Christ fundamentally involves how I treat other people, especially other people who are members of my church? Have I covenanted together to love them, and do I give myself to that?

Or, have you claimed that you know a love from God in Christ and yet live in a way that contradicts that claim? Do you claim that you know this kind of love that knows no bounds, and yet in loving others you set bounds, saying in effect, "I'll go this far but no further"?

Such a claim to love, without a life backing it up, is a bad sign. And yet, if you just hang out by yourself and refuse to join a church, other Christians can't help you. You're sailing your own little ship your own little way. You'll come to church when you like the sermons, you'll come when you like the music or when you like something else that the church does, then you'll sail on out to wherever else you may go when you want something else.

Membership in a local church is not an antiquated, outdated, unnecessary add-on to true membership in the universal body of Christ; membership in a local church is intended to be a testimony to our membership in the universal church. Church membership does not save, but it reflects salvation. And if there is no reflection of our salvation, how can we be sure that we are truly saved? As John explains, "If anyone says, 'I love God,' yet hates his brother, he is a liar. For anyone who does not love his brother, whom he has seen, cannot love God, whom he has not seen" (1 John 4:20).

In becoming a member of the church, we are grasping hands with each other to know and be known by each other. We are agreeing to help and encourage each other when we need to be reminded of God's work in our lives or when we need to be challenged about major discrepancies between our talk and our walk.

6) Join a Church to Expose False Gospels

As we interact with other Christians, we show the world what Christianity really is; we dispel the false notion that Christians are nauseatingly self-righteous people who are worried that someone somewhere might be having fun and who believe, above all else, in their own goodness. Many non-Christians view Christianity this way. We can combat that false image by having a church that is not marked by such an attitude.

Some years ago, I visited a relative whom I hadn't seen since childhood. My announcement that I was planning to be a Baptist preacher didn't go over very well. She paused, looked down at her coffee, and said, "I've given up on organized religion. I think I've decided that churches are just pits of vipers."

"Really?" I replied.

"Yep," she said.

"Do you really think the world outside is so much better?" I asked.

She thought for a second: "Well, I guess not. They're vipers too. But at least they know they're vipers."

I said, "You might be surprised how much I agree with you. I know the world outside is a pit of vipers. And I know the church is a pit of vipers too. But the difference is, I don't really think the world outside knows that they are. And I think Christians know that they are, and that's why we go to church—because we know we need help. Because we know that we're dependent on God and that we're saved by his grace alone."

All we can bring to our salvation is our sin. It must be God's love in Christ that saves us. He came and lived a perfect life for us, died on the cross in place of all those who would ever turn and trust in him, and rose in victory over death and over sin. Our faith in him alone is the instrument by which we are saved.

So join a church that believes in that gospel. Join with other Christians in covenant membership to make that truth known.

7) Join a Church to Glorify God

Finally, if you are a Christian, you should join a church for the glory of God. Peter wrote to some early Christians, "Live such good lives among the pagans that, though they accuse you of doing wrong, they may see your good deeds and glorify God on the day he visits us" (1 Pet. 2:12).

Amazing, isn't it? You can tell that Peter had heard the teaching of his Master. Remember what Jesus taught in the Sermon on the Mount: "Let your light shine before men, that they may see your good deeds and praise your Father in heaven" (Matt. 5:16).

Again, the surprising assumption seems to be that God will get the glory for our good deeds. If that is true of our lives individually, it shouldn't surprise us that it is also true of our lives together as Christians. God intends that the way we love each other will identify us as followers of Christ. Recall Jesus's words in John 13:34–35: "A new command I give you: Love one another. As I have loved you, so you must love one another. By this all men will know that you are my disciples, if you love one another."

Our lives together are to mark us out as his and are to bring him praise and glory.

Jesus said, "I will build my church" (Matt. 16:18). If Jesus is committed to the church, should we be any less committed to it?

Most Christians who regularly attend a God-centered, Bible-preaching church feel frustration at some point. But remember, all families have issues. Those moments of frustration are precisely the times when we can exercise forgiveness, walk in patience, and love others who may have nothing to give us in return. These committed, covenant church relationships will bring glory to God.

Commit to the Body of Christ

In the next-to-the-last scene of Robert Bolt's play *A Man for All Seasons*, Thomas More's daughter, Meg, comes to his cell to convince him to say what he needs to say in order to free himself. Meg pleads, "Then say the words of the oath and in your heart, think otherwise."

"Well, . . . finally," says More, "it isn't a matter of reason; finally it's a matter of love."[1]

Joining a particular local church is an outward reflection of an inward love—for Christ and for his people. And, as we see so often in this life, the greatest love is rarely merely spontaneous; it is more often planned, premeditated, and characterized by commitment.

Ephesians 5:25 says that "Christ loved the church and gave himself up for her." Acts 20:28 reminds us that he bought his church with his own blood. If we are Christ's followers, we too should love the church that he gave himself for.

So, do not merely attend a church (though you should attend) but join a church. Link arms with other Christians. Find a church you can join, and do it so that non-Christians will hear and see the gospel, so that weak Christians will be cared for, so that strong Christians will channel their energies in a good way, so that church leaders will be encouraged and helped, and so that God will be glorified.

Recommended Resources

Thabiti Anyabwile, *What Is a Healthy Church Member?* (Wheaton, IL: Crossway, 2008).

Mark Dever, *Nine Marks of a Healthy Church* (Wheaton, IL: Crossway, 2013).

Jonathan Leeman, *Church Membership: How the World Knows Who Represents Jesus* (Wheaton, IL: Crossway, 2012).

Notes

1. Robert Bolt, *A Man for All Seasons* (New York: Random House, 1990), 141.

Scripture Index

Scripture Index

IX 9Marks

Building Healthy Churches

9Marks exists to equip church leaders with a biblical vision and practical resources for displaying God's glory to the nations through healthy churches.

To that end, we want to see churches characterized by these nine marks of health:

1. Expositional Preaching
2. Gospel Doctrine
3. A Biblical Understanding of Conversion and Evangelism
4. Biblical Church Membership
5. Biblical Church Discipline
6. A Biblical Concern for Discipleship and Growth
7. Biblical Church Leadership
8. A Biblical Understanding of the Practice of Prayer
9. A Biblical Understanding and Practice of Missions

Find all our Crossway titles and other resources at 9Marks.org.

9Marks | Church Questions

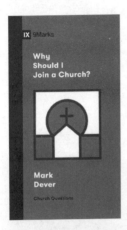
IX 9Marks

Why
Should I
Join a Church?

Mark
Dever

Church Questions

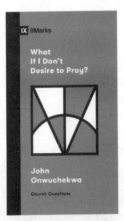
IX 9Marks

What
If I Don't
Desire to Pray?

John
Onwuchekwa

Church Questions

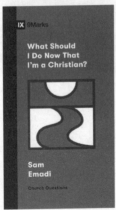
IX 9Marks

What Should
I Do Now That
I'm a Christian?

Sam
Emadi

Church Questions

IX 9Marks

What If I'm
Discouraged
in My Evangelism?

Isaac
Adams

Church Questions

crossway.org